Anonymous

Douglas' doctrine of popular sovereignty in the territories;

Its counterpart

Anonymous

Douglas' doctrine of popular sovereignty in the territories;
Its counterpart

ISBN/EAN: 9783337818753

Printed in Europe, USA, Canada, Australia, Japan

Cover: Foto ©ninafisch / pixelio.de

More available books at **www.hansebooks.com**

OF

POPULAR SOVEREIGNTY

IN THE TERRITORIES;

ITS

COUNTERPART.

———— • • ————

BY A MISSOURIAN.

——

ST. LOUIS;
PRINTED BY R. V. KENNEDY & COMPANY,
OFFICE OF THE CITY DIRECTORY.

————

1860.

In respect to the thoughtfulness and resolve with which he has received and advocated the views and plan of Mr. Jefferson, on the subject of Negro Colonization—a question of importance to the white and black races in the Union, involving material interests of the highest order to the one, and of humanity to the other; and which, from the very fact of its pure and unmixed usefulness, elicits the usual opposition that arises and confronts the benefit of the people.

MR. DOUGLAS' DOCTRINE

OF

POPULAR SOVEREIGNTY

IN THE TERRITORIES;

ITS

COUNTERPART.

BY A MISSOURIAN.

———◦◇◦◦———

The views of Mr. Douglas, in elucidation of the principle of Popular Sovereignty, are given in the September number of Harper's Magazine; the article is elaborate, and contains all the facts and reasoning that can probably be advanced in its support. We may safely rely, that upon this exposition the Senator places himself in defence of his doctrine of "Squatter Sovereignty." If the basis be substantial, in conformity with the faithful interpretation of Constitutional provision, Mr. Douglas has done eminent service to the Nation, for which he should be well remembered—if, on the other hand, facts are strained and disjointed, and a perverted, nay, corrupt interpretation of Constitutional Law is manifest therein, upon analysis, the necessary result follows, of disappointment commensurate with the design, and the loss of faith in the opinion of the people— the most fatal blight in our country to the prospects of a public man.

The importance of a political subject is usually considered a just ground for amplification in its treatment. Mr. Douglas' treatise has the merit of extensive research. Yet take away the magnitude of the matter, and the facts bearing upon it are few, and the reasoning manifest; the Senator, however, having concluded otherwise, has treated the subject with a large array of statement, the application of which is more than ambiguous. I do not deny, but am pleased to acknowledge, that the gentle-man has evinced varied tact and wariness in his arrangement. He states the position of the Republican Party on the Constitutional power of Congress over the Territories, and of the right and duty of Congress, in the exercise of that power, to prohibit, among other things, slavery therein, in the language of their Convention; he places the doctrine of the National Democracy in the line of irreconcilable opposition thereto, but admits it would be uncandid to deny that there are radical differences of opinion in that party, respecting the powers and duties of Congress, and the rights and immunities of the people of the Territories under the Federal Constitution, (on the subject of Slavery.) He then divides the National Democracy into three segments, upon the proper construction of the constitutional provision touching the powers of Congress over Slavery in the Territories; and after ignoring the interpretation of two of them, he declares himself, as usual, in favor of the following, as the Constitutional doctrine :

First: Those who believe that the Constitution of the United States neither establishes nor prohibits Slavery in the States or Territories beyond the power of the people legally to control it, but 'leaves the people thereof perfectly free to form and regulate their domestic institutions in their own way, subject only to the Constitution of the United States.'

Having given his reasoning in antagonism to the interpreta-tion that the Constitution establishes Slavery in the Territories, to be vindicated as some of the National Democracy contend, either by the Territorial Legislature, or, in lack thereof, by Congress, or by the Judiciary, by virtue of Constitutional authority, and independent of any Legislative action whatever, as by some leaders of the Democracy is proclaimed, Mr. Douglas settles down to an array of facts and reasoning in support of his construction of the Constitution. Such is the plan of the treatise; he states and opposes the the conven-tional views of the Republican party—he wipes away the ultra interpretation of those of the Democracy who maintain that the Constitution creates Slavery in the Territories, either by subordinate Legislation, or, *proprio vigore ;* and concludes that the people of a Territory, and no other authority, have, under the Constitution, the right to regulate the question. Such is the system of his address, plain enough when analysed and stripped of various excrescences that profusely surround it.

From this it appears that any one who differs with Mr. Douglas need have no care of defending, except incidentally, the Republican Doctrine—that Doctrine is now the assailant, and Mr. Douglas is on the defense. Having defeated, as he deems, the interpretation of the Republican Party in Congress by the Compromise Acts of 1850–54, he sits entrenched within the fortress of a Legislative section and invites attack. The proper course then is to simplify proceedings—omitting, except of necessity, any vindication of the interpretation by the Republican party, of the Constitutional right of Congress over the question of Slavery in the Territories, and much more, neglecting altogether the intemperate views of that portion of his own party, which Mr. Douglas himself proclaims unsound, let us analyze the facts and reasoning of the Senator, and award him the result of impartial justice.

One difficulty, however, presents itself at the outset, which ought not to exist—the language of Mr. Douglas' proposition is informal and obscure—nay, it is worse, but I prefer moderation; in grave proceedings, however, of momentous import, this is unpardonable; and yet, if we rectify the language of the Senator, what will become of his reasoning? Read his first classification as above, and insert between the words "but" and "leaves", to make the sentence sense, the words "that it" (viz : the Constitution of the United States,) and the Senator has made a rich bequest to the Nation, in the following unparalleled conclusion of his proposition : "First: Those who believe that the Constitution of the United States neither establishes nor prohibits Slavery in the States or Territories beyond the power of the people legally to control it, but (that it, the Constitution of the United States,) leaves the people thereof perfectly free to form and regulate their domestic institutions in their own way, subject only to the Constitution of the United States." Such is the written wisdom of Senator Douglas, and to so ripe a conclusion does he lead his readers. I know the force of early education, and I can pardon its dialectics. Here, in the West, the Creole expression, "*cul de sac*," has been applied to a section of country once so entangled that he who was unlucky enough to enter it, could not find his way out; and if the Constitution of the United States, according to Mr. Douglas' parlance, is so liberal as to give the people of a Territory perfect freedom to form and regulate the domestic institution of Slavery in their own way, subject only to the restrictions contained in that Constitution, I cannot see how the gentleman escapes the position of the western wight who first found himself in "*the bottom of the bag.*" If the true construction of the Constitution be, that the people of a Territory have nothing to say on the subject, except by authority of

Congress, through their Territorial Legislature, what is the amount of this gift of perfect freedom so loudly harped upon? But even the first part of his proposition is peculiar, and, I fear, places the Senator in a worse dilemma. It would be strange if the true interpretation of it cancelled his petted theory. Mr. Douglas belongs to that class of the National Democracy "who believe that the Constitution of the United States neither establishes nor prohibits Slavery in the States or Territories, beyond the power of the people legally to control it," the converse whereof asserts, in unmistakable meaning, that the Constitution establishes or prohibits Slavery in the States or Territories at will, but *within the power of the people legally to control it ;* thus he admits, in his own proposition, the Constitutional right to regulate the subject of Slavery not only in the Territories, but (tell it not South,) in the States, where, when it exists, it is a legal institution, that no Republican dreams of disturbing. *The power of the people legally to control slavery* is impotent surplusage, idle to introduce into a controverted subject, and partaking largely of scenic clap-trap—has it not always, until within a few years, existed without question or mooting?—have not the people of South Carolina, to-day, the right to control Slavery legally, and expel it from their borders if they choose? But how can the Constitutional provision, thus, as Mr. Douglas admits, establishing or prohibiting slavery in the Territories, (I omit States, in mercy to the gentleman,) be enforced, except by Congressional action, and have not the people of a Territory in their election of a Legislature, (as is uniformly followed,) full power over the subject of Slavery, as over every other subject matter that interests them locally? I but glance here at the results which legitimately follow from the logical interpretation of the language of the Senator; they are radiant with hope, and if the mildest of the Democratic sections, led on by a man of energy and ambition, in the well-poised sentence that concentrates and embodies his construction of the Constitution, find that they are marshalled under false colors, and are marching North, too far North, when told, in the loud tones of their leader, that their step and mission are South, these gentlemen, a numerous body, untinged with fanaticism, and obedient only to the will of the Constitution, will pause and retreat from the covert ambush of Mr. Douglas' favorite proposition.

But let us try to disregard language, and vindicate the Senator's intent, however expressed. Except he beguiles us and seeks to delude our virgin judgment, Mr. Douglas means to inform the Nation that the Constitution of the United

States confers no power upon Congress to interfere with the question of Slavery in the States or Territories whatever, but that the people thereof, and they alone, control it—I omit the words "*subject only to the Constitution of the United States,*" for if Mr. Douglas is sincere, they are inapposite. Doubtless Congress, under the Constitution, has the right of yea or nay when a Territory applies for admission as a State, but, except in this instance, which he cannot deny, and which leaves him in a dread position, his theory excludes all Congressional interference. This is the only doctrine I can unravel from his circumlocution, and although subtlety has varied resources, and can conveniently change the complexion and meaning of a proposition indifferently expressed, sometimes for a purpose, I submit to the public if this is not the true intent of the doctrine of Squatter Sovereignty?

When the gentleman interposed the words "subject only to the Constitution of the United States," why not elucidate his exception, by declaring, in a word, in addition thereto, where, in the Constitution, the provision lies, that makes the action of the people in a Territory or State, on the question of Slavery, subject to its control. If the people of a Territory are perfectly free to form and regulate their domestic institution of Slavery by leave of the Constitution, as Mr. Douglas reiterates, should he not be careful to point out where the subjection of this perfect freedom is implied or expressed in the Supreme Law—what is its amount and limit? In the absence of such authority, which he has not adduced, and cannot, I will treat this language as it merits, in considering the meaning of a political proposition of an American States-man—I will pass it without notice—for among other reasons, if the Constitution of the United States subjects the perfect freedom of the people of a State or Territory to form and regulate their domestic institution of Slavery in their own way, to restriction, it necessarily establishes or prohibits Slavery therein at pleasure. If such be the result, what becomes of the Senator's hallucination? I shall, therefore, omit noticing it, out of respect to the subject, or, if I touch upon it again, it shall be when it may perchance benefit the Senator, if possible—nor would it do to allow a national mischief to have any chance of further existence.

Mr. Douglas' doctrine then, the true meaning of the proposition in his first classification, which he upholds and embellishes, apart from any redundancy of words that have no application, or if any, one fatal to his purpose, is, that under the Constitution, the people of a State or Territory are perfect freemen to form and regulate their domestic institution of Slavery in their own way. To elucidate this, without any necessity, he addresses himself with varied historical learning, Colonial, Revolutionary and National. In a series of facts, recited from the history of of the Colonies, Virginia especially, he maintains the distinction that he draws in the first place between Federal and Local authority, and argues that while the Colonies, to the very last, implicitly yielded imperial authority to Great Britain, they still insisted upon their right of making their own local laws, forming their own domestic institutions and managing their own internal affairs, Slavery included, in their own way, subject only to the English Constitution, as the paramount law of the Empire.

He further avers that the Colonies recognized and conceded to the Imperial Government all general powers, including the right to institute their government, by *granting* charters, under which, the inhabitants residing within the limits of any specified territory, might be organized into a political community, with a government consisting of its appropriate departments, executive, legislative and judicial; but that conceding all these powers, the Colonies emphatically denied that the Imperial Government had any rightful authority to impose taxes upon them without their consent, or to interfere with their internal polity—claiming that it was the birthright of all Englishmen, inalienable, when formed into a political community, to exercise and enjoy all the rights privileges and immunities of self-government, in respect to all matters and things, which were local and not general, internal and not external, Colonial and not Imperial, as fully as if they were inhabitants of England, with a fair representation in Parliament. The statement proceeds to say "that our fathers of the Revolution were contending, not for independence in the first instance, but for the inestimable right of local self-government under the British Constitution—the right of every distinct political community, dependent Colonies, Territories, and Provinces, as well as sovereign States, to make their own local laws, form their own domestic institutions, and manage their own internal affairs in their own way, subject only to the Constitution of Great Britain, as the paramount law of the Empire;" further "the Government of Great Britain had violated this inalienable right of local self-government by a long series of acts on a great variety of subjects."

I rescue myself here from the tedium of further quotation, so prolific of the style peculiar to Mr. Douglas, and which, being his own, differs materially from the synopsis of the

9

argument in favor of the Compromise Act of 1850, which he extracts and condenses in his defense, and to which he puts in a surreptitious claim of *quasi*, that is at once repudiated by the luminous language of Mr. Clay. He sought to conciliate the Nation upon a morbid subject, but was yet too pure, even for the highest object of human ambition, to interpolate the text of the Constitution, or give it intentionally a false gloss. I will cheerfully yield to the weight of the inferential reasoning of the Senator, whatever he claims for it fairly, if the facts of Colonial remonstrance on the subject of Slavery, and the tyranny of the British crown in answer thereto, be correctly stated, which I deny. A parallel is drawn between the Constitution and Government of Great Britain and her American Colonies, (differing in legislation on the matter of Slavery,) on the one side, and the Constitution and Congress of this Union and the rights of the people of its Territories therein, on the other; and the inference drawn is, that the constant struggle of the Colonial Legislatures against the interference of the British crown, contrary to the Constitution of England and the rights of the Colonies as defined in their Charters, being facts well known to the Congress of 1774, induced them to include the following among the series of their resolutions : " That they are entitled to a free and exclusive power in their several Provincial Legislatures, where their right of representation can alone be preserved, in all cases of taxation and internal polity :" and that, therefore, because of this resolution, and still more because of the action of the Federal Convention of 1787, which formed the present Constitution, wherein the dividing line between Federal and Local authority, in respect to Terrtories, was distinctly marked, it is patent, that in all the Legislation, inchoate, progressive, or final, connected with the Constitution, it could not have been within the intent of these organic founders to introduce therein any provision authorizing the interference of Congress on the subject of Slavery in the Territories.

The attempt to draw a parallel between Great Britain and her Colonies, and the United States and her Territories, is not only infelicitous, but positively offensive. Can the Senator point out where, in the British Constitution, any letter breathes the distinction which he so fancifully draws between imperial and local rights in the Colonies? can he lead us to any provision the most faint in the Colonial charters (mere patents of several kings, given and revoked at pleasure, yielding no inalienable birthrights, as Mr. Douglas mockingly intimates,) which segregates the local rights of the Colonies from the general privileges of the crown? Can he produce any act of the British Parliament—whose legislation the Senator should be informed was the supreme law, overruling, at pleasure, this British Constitution that he so tastefully puts in juxta position with the Constitution of our country—suspending at will the Habeas Corpus Act, the right of trial by jury, and other component parts of this mythical *sex inscripta*, can he adduce any act of this supreme authority, during our Colonial existence, that conferred one jot or tittle of privilege upon or recognized an inalienable right of any American Colony, independent of the parent power? If such things do not exist, what becomes of his statement that the Revolution was based upon the non-recognition, by England, of the inalienable local rights of the Colonies, when they had none; why, after a bare mention of the imposition of taxes without the consent of the payer, does he studiously avoid the fundamental cause of the Revolution, (taxation without representation,) and lay the burden of that weighty movement upon the subordinate question of local rights, that did not legally exist, and never were declared inalienable, until the American Charter arose. Does he term the taxation, against which the Colonies rebelled, an internal and not an external matter? and if by compulsion he is forced to admit it an imperial impost, against which the Colonies had no objection save one, viz : the denial to them of a voice in the laying of it, either in the Parliament of Great Britain, by their representatives there, or by the confirmatory vote of the local Legislature, how does he affirm it, that the interference by England with what he calls the internal polity of the Colonies, (the Slavery question,) was not treated by her and resisted by them, as an imperial right? Will it be said that the dividing line between Federal and Local authority was ever heard of, much less legalized, in any government of the world, before the demarcation was first drawn by the Colonists and solemnly affirmed in the Constitutions of the United States? That it was mooted and canvassed in the Colonies, is obvious, as every other subject of political right was treated—but it was merely embryotic and invasive, novel and revolutionary, never recognized, but on the contrary scorned and abhorred by Mr. Douglas' model Government of Great Britain, from whom we derive, quoth he, our political theory and system, as he delineates in such exact parallel. The privileges of the English Charters were all that legally belonged to the Colonies, and of these, whatever they were, they were only tenants at will—not a ray of political right illuminates these dreary documents—they dole out petty powers as a miser dispenses small charity, while he grasps the real treasures with a death hold. It is an incomprehensible slight to the intelligence of the Nation, that the productive rights of States and Territories, as authoritatively enunciated in the Federal Constitution, and bearing the impress of perpetuity, should be indecently trifled with, by an elaborate assimilation with the barren grants to the Colonies, contained in the Charters of their kings, arbitrary as they were, and revocable at will. Is not history an open page, and can its facts be altered by Mr. Douglas' declamation? the American Revolution was based not upon any violation by England of rights and privileges by her conferred upon the Colonies, and which she afterwards interdicted them in the exercise of, but upon the utter abnegation and tyrannous denial to her Colonial subjects of a right (representative taxation,) which was enjoyed by her people at home, aided and abetted by her stern refusal to the Colonies, of the exercise of certain other rights, which they claimed to be, first just, finally inalienable, of dealing, for instance, with the domestic question of Slavery—to use the gentleman's familiar, not to say homely language—*in their own way.* These Charters were not even the true representatives of value—they were more honest on their face, however, than the Senator's interpretation of them; he reads them as containing the gold and silver standard of the Constitution of our country—what a mockery! They were tested by truer alchemists, Mr. Jefferson for one, and pronounced base, whereupon they were seized and destroyed by the iron hand of the Revolution.

The Senator can take nothing by this adroit attempt at inferential aid from the preliminary quarrels, the war of words, between England and the Colonies. There is no paternity in the descent of a political right, which, though claimed and embryotic, was never in existence, towards one that can be plainly found living in a written Constitution—neither are we required to understand the voice or silence of an instrument, by the light of preliminary facts, so dim and indistinct as to render its characters cabalistic. Mr. Douglas cannot deceive the American people into the belief that, because England would not permit the Colony of Virginia to check and restrain the policy of negro importation and increase, "by the inhuman use of the Royal negative," the framers of the Constitution, therefore, would be deterred from inserting, in that instrument, a provision authorizing the very right which the Colonies claimed. He cannot wrench the facts of Colonial history from their true application, although he will not take them, so to speak, as they come, nor has he the power to extract from the disjointed statement any reasoning in aid of his wry inferences, which even a gownsman cannot dissipate. I pass from this attempt at inferential aid, in behalf of the doctrine of "Squatter Sovereignty," by virtue of the effect of our Colonial history, conceived with a shrewdness and treated with a transparency altogether worthy of the gentleman's capacity.

The Constitution provides, that "Congress shall have power to dispose of, and make all needful rules and regulations respecting the Territories, or other property belonging to the United States;" this is a provision that has some bearing on the subject of territorial treatment—the import of the term "Territory," the extent and scope of its meaning become then essential to understand the object of this Constitutional provision. Mr. Douglas strenuously advocates that it shall be interpreted according to the understanding of the day in which it was first used. Why should he dread any knavish abuse of the word? it had never been used or understood, says he, at the time the Constitution was framed, to designate a political community or government of any kind, in any law, compact, deed of session or public document, but had invariably been used in its geographical sense, to describe the superficial area of a state or district of country, as in the Virginia Deed of Cession of the "*territory or tract of country,*" Northwest of the River Ohio; or, as meaning land in its character of property, in which latter sense it appears in this clause of the Constitution when providing for the disposition of the "territory or other property belonging to the United States." These facts, says he, taken in connection with the kindred one, that during the whole period of the Confederation and the formation of the Constitution, *the temporary governments,* which we now call territories, were invariably referred to in the deeds of cession, laws, compacts, plans of government, resolutions of Congress, public records and authentic documents, (the Statesman is as profuse as a country attorney,) as States, or "new States," conclusively show that the words "territory and other property," in the Constitution, were used to designate the unappropriated lands and other property which the United States owned, and not the people who might become residents on those lands, and be organized into political communities after the United States had parted with their title." The meaning of all which crowded verbiage is that in the year 1787, when the Constitution was constructed, the term "territory" meant land in its character of property, and did not designate a political community or government of any kind. Such is the definition that pleases Mr. Douglas, and although a very limited one,

yet, for this instance, it pleases us also. But, as it appears by
Mr. Douglas, there were in those days temporary governments,
now by us called Territories, then, that is, during the whole
period of the Confederation and the formation of the Constitution (from 1778 to 1787,) known and referred to as States,
or new States, I would enquire of the gentleman, from what
source these governmental formations arose? But was there any
Territorial organization in existence from 1778 to 1787, the
period he quotes—if there was none, and if the origin of our
government is not yet lost, like that of the Roman, in fable,
and never will be, I foretell, except Mr. Douglas assumes the
character of its historian, what becomes of his interpretation
of a provision that had its existence in the future, and did not
operate on the present or the past, for the reason that there
were none. If they were in existence, it must be by some
authority, and where, except in this provision, is that authority
to be found. This power, granted Congress by the Constitution,
was the first born offspring of a new order of political necessity;
it was never needed before, and was given at the proper time
as an authority to govern the future. Many political organizations having sprung up since 1787, not called States, or
" new States"—which never did exist, except in Mr. Douglas'
mythology—but Territories, as the term is now understood by
the people of this country, and was always understood from
the beginning of the formation of the governmental organizations called Territories, I am here prepared to enquire, if the
Senator is prepared to answer, how and by what authority,
except of this provision of the Constitution, these solemn
governmental organizations were created. This clause, according to his statement, merely grants Congress an auctioneer's
license to cry its lands, or the authority of a peddler to
dispose of its governmental rubbish. I always thought,
however, that the ownership of property implied the right of
adjustment, transfer and sale, without the aid of a provision of
the Constitution of the United States to justify it—but I will
yield it, to accommodate the Senator; if he struggles
to humiliate and dishonor the bright Charter of American
Rights, I will accompany him any distance, until he
reap the full reward of his impiety. If the Constitution was scrupulously careful to provide for the meanest
details of the Territorial household, its authors must have
been singularly provident and elaborate, in regard to the
birth and nurture of the occupant. These republican nurse-
lings were dearer in the eyes of the stern patriots of the
Revolution, than all the baby progeny of kings. The Constitu-

tion was to be the text book from which the Federal Government and its administrators were to draw their instructions for territorial management. Mr. Douglas admits, strange to say, that the provision empowering Congress to institute temporary governments for the new States, arising in the unappropriated lands of the United States, submitted by Mr. Madison in the Convention and referred to the proper committee, was afterwards embodied and now exists as a power in the Constitution. I demand of him where, in the Constitution, if not in this needful rule and regulation clause, where he all but swears it does not exist—if not there, where then, thou embodiment of consistency and logic! Those Revolutionary sires, whom the gentleman never lets slip the opportunity of piously lauding, with the calm unction and affected sigh of a faded beauty, who lives by what she lost, must have been very heartless fathers, in making no provision for the legitimate offspring of the country; yet, after all, the founders of the Constitution were not these improvident progenitors, nor are the Territories foundlings, as Senator Douglas would cruelly inform them—they are the decendents and co-heirs of the general government, raised and protected by its parent hand, according to the letter and spirit of this Constitutional provision, without which there was no connecting tie, no family link between the relatives—the Constitution makes the Territory a child of the Federal Government and an inheritor of State rights—the doctrine of "Squatter Sovereignty," like the spirit of evil, for an unholy purpose, would originate strife between child and parent, exile the stripling from the threshold and hearth of its founder, invent where it could not find, stubbornly deny where it could not overlook, palliate and avert where it must meet, and mystify where it could not blot out; and all this, with a bluster of patriotism, and an air of disinterested love of the public, that naturally befits Mr. Douglas.

A distinction is sought to be drawn between the amount of Congressional authority, legal in the Territories, and that over the District, the seat of the government of the United States, from the difference of language used in the Constitution. The right of the exercise of exclusive legislation, in all cases whatsoever, over the District of Columbia, and all places in the States, where the general Government erected needful buildings, forts, magazines, &c., makes the difference, it is said, in the powers, and draws the line between Federal and Municipal authority. Sovereignty, wherever placed, is a unit, and retains all it vast proportions naturally, except when shorn thereof in part by express original compact; limited sovereignty is the

distinctive theory of our system, and the great extent to which
we have carried it, has worked wonders in the good government of men; it is an American invention, the patenting of
which cost profusely, but it pays better than the discovery of
the needle, the art of printing, electricity, or the cotton gin;
the language which embodies this vital principle must be
construed with the utmost circumspection, nor yet its intent
reached with any niggard hand; above all it must be preserved
sacred from the taint of causistry. When the provision in
the Constitution, concerning the mode of government, whatever it is, of the Territories and the District, were enacted,
there was no Territorial organization in being, and the District
land was not yet acquired of the States; the Constitutional
provisions were, therefore, prospective in their operation; the
species of provision that was applicable to a District, was not,
however, applicable to a Territory—in process of time, the
Territory would become a State, which form the District could
never assume, under any circumstances—hence the separate
provisions and the difference in them—the one provides for a
permanent organization, the other for a transitory form of
government; besides, the Constitution erected the Federal
Government by subtracting from State sovereignties certain
attributes, which loss, the Territories, when they lapsed into
States, should also encounter; a condition that need not at all
be regarded in the case of the District—her fate was final, that
of a Territory diurnal—hence a necessary difference of Constitutional provision—The exercise of exclusive legislation, in
all cases, whatever, over the District—being an unrestricted
petty sovereignty, differing from the State and Federal sovereignties, as defined and limited, elsewhere, in the Constitution
—is granted expressly, to guard it forever, as it was a perpetuity,
from such analogies as those of Mr. Douglas; but, in the case
of Territories, the undisputed sovereignty therein, that
enured instanter to the Federal Government the moment she
acquired the soil, as, for instance, the gift from Virginia, in
1784, remained paramount and intact by Constitutional
restriction, it being beside the necessity of the case, to
interfere with the solemn right of sovereignty for a transient
and fleeting occasion; hence Federal power in the District of
Columbia and the localities of forts, arsenals, &c., is marked
out distinctly, being an exclusive power, different from any
other in the Constitution; and hence, also, Federal power in
the Territories, without its sovereignty therein being at all
questioned, is required in the general language befitting the
case, " to dispose of the territory, or other property, belonging

to the United States, and to make all needful rules and regulations respecting the same," being nothing more, whilst it endorses the absolute inherent sovereignty in the Federal Government over the Territories, in the most comprehensive terms, than pointing out how that sovereignty should be exercised by "Congressional Legislation"—analyse the provision : "Congress shall have power to dispose of the Territory belonging to the United States"—"dispose"—does the language furnish a more comprehensive term for the purpose; perhaps, in the copiousness of his diction, the Senator could supply it—but Mr. Madison, who was not given to wordiness, selected it as the apposite term "to authorize Congress to institute temporary governments for the new States"—nay, so absolute is the aspect in which this and its kindred language in the provision regards the sovereignty of the Federal Government over the Territories, that the terms employed "*dispose*" —"*rules and regulations*," is the language used by the Autocrat respecting his serf, and the master of his slave—you are not compelled even to legislate for them—*sic volo sic jubeo*. It is admitted that Mr. Madison submitted to the Constitutional Convention, as of certain powers, the one "to institute temporary government for the new States," and that the provision, of which we are treating, was the result of this proposition, or, in the words of Mr. Douglas, "here we find the original and rough draft of these several powers as they now exist in their revised form in the Constitution." What sense of public honor then belongs to the corrupt assertion that this clause of the Constitution merely confers power on Congress "to provide for the survey and sale of the land, military sites, old ships, cannon, muskets, or other property, real or personal, which belonged to the United States, and are no longer needful for any public purpose?" Of equal decency—also, that is, in defiance of all decency, is the following reputable statement, "such a power, had it been vested in Congress, would annihilate the svereoignty and freedom of the States, as well as the principle of self government in the Territories wherever the United States happened to own a portion of the public lands within their respective limits, as at present, in several States and Territories," (enumerating twenty of them.) To what shifts political, like other crime, drives its votaries; Mr. Douglas, having doggedly affixed a vicious interpretation to the Constitutional text, is compelled to take refuge in the States, in order to justify his version of a provision, which he himself admits, was prepared by Mr. Madison and embodied in the Constitution only for the Territories, and here in this notable passage contends that his interpretation is conclusive, because, if the owner of property in a State, (the Federal Government, for instance,) exercises the right of ownership by selling it, a right that is inherent, and needs no law to authorize its exercise, the sovereignty and freedom of the State are annihilated and the great principle of self-government in the Territories is ruined; he has taken refuge in the States, a fugitive for the crime committed in the Territories, and I here invoke the aid of the Constitutional provision to reclaim him.

The Senator is rather partial to political inuendo; when he finds himself stripped of all direct authority in the Constitution to invest a Territory with the insignia of government, after he weakly abandons the only provision that furnishes them, he falls back upon the mysteries of inference and the power of comparison—"the provision," says he, "to authorize Congress to institute temporary governments for the new States or Territories and to provide for their admission into the Union, appears in the Constitution in this form, "new States may be admitted by Congress into this Union,"—"the power," he continues, "to admit *new States*" and to make all laws which shall be necessary and proper to that end, may fairly be construed to include the right to institute temporary governments for such new States or Territories, the same as Great Britain could rightfully institute similar governments for the Colonies, but certainly not to authorize Congress to legislate in respect to their municipal affairs and internal concerns, without violating that great fundamental principle, in defence of which the battles of the Revolution were fought." Mr. Douglas, knowing that Territorial governments have been created by Congress under the sanction of the Constitution, sets out with a firm resolve to lose the authority where it exists, and to find it where it is not. The 3rd Section of the fourth Article of the Instrument has two subdivisions in very few words—in these lines the power is comprised, or nowhere; Phocion could not have written them more succinctly, nor Tacitus more terse—in fact, a greater than the Greek for brevity, or the historian for clearness, composed the simple words that create and govern those infant empires. But Mr. Douglas waywardly selects the creating for the governing power; he will not accept the truth, no more than the mistress her gift, except indirectly. The power to admit new States, and (grant him his interpolation,) to make all laws which shall be necessary and proper to that end, may not fairly be construed to include the right to institute temporary governments for such new States or

Territories under any circumstances. The power to admit is totally distinct from the power to govern; the one is of form, the other of substance. According to Mr. Douglas' version, we may as well as aught else read his reasoning, as authorizing Congress to institute governments for the infant State, after its admission. But, although the statesman reasons as the worsted Athlete fought, wildly, I cannot, for the honor of the Presidency, allow the candidate to perpetrate the blunder of a Driveller. Mr. Douglas surely means that the power of Congress to admit an organized Territory into the family of States, after having reached a certain grade of maturity, including numbers of inhabitants, proper form of State Constitution, application and requirement, although an Act of finality, which terminated the territorial life, and gave another existence to the community, included, also, the right to exercise, not a subsequent or inferential, but a prior function of power, viz, to govern the Territories, as England did her Colonies, with a discrimination in favor of municipal and internal legislation; still this is bad reasoning; even the schools pronounce it so. Were it the contrary case, there would be a vivid show of reason for him in the absence of Constitutional provision. If the Constitution omitted all mention of the power of Congress to admit new States, endorsing as it does the inherent power of the Federal Authority to institute temporary governments for the Territories, the inferential argument of the gentleman would be valid, because the Territorial government, form and style, were only temporary, and must necessarily ripen into the majority of State existence; but a Territory may well be admitted by Congress Constitutionally into the Union as a State, without its ever having had any concern with the Territorial mode of life, in case the Constitution were silent on the subject. And, in fact, although the Constitution declares how the Territory is to be governed by Congress, when the soil belongs to the Union, yet, such is the liberality of construction properly given to this power of the admission of new States, that even when the territory, that is the soil composing one, never before belonged to the Federal Government, it is still unhesitatingly admitted by Congress upon proper application. What becomes of Mr. Douglas' inferential power of Congress to govern a Territory, from the right of admission of new States, in the case of Texas? Did this Government own the soil of the Territory previously, or exercise any jurisdiction there? Such is the humiliation to which a wilful misconstruction of one Constitutional provision, and an unnatural construction of another, reduce the argument of the gentleman—Hence flow those political fancies by which he pretends to instruct and vindicate the people: from such source is derived "Popular Sovereignty," the lineal descendant of the principle in dispute between Great Britain and the Colonies, now resurrected by Mr. Douglas, as a cause of quarrel between this Union and her Territories. What a debt of obligation does he not owe Great Britain? her tyranny not only occasioned the Revolution, but it has even made Senator Douglas a prominent man—it obliterated the dividing line between General and Municipal Governments, which was insisted upon as a fundamental principle, in defense of which the battles of the Revolution were fought, and it has furnished the gentleman, tyranny though it was, with his great fundamental principle of "Squatter Sovereignty" in defense of which the battles of the Presidential Campaign are being fought. The jealousy of our people has been often aroused at the idea of British interference in our elections, yet Mr. Douglas reposes all his hopes of the Presidency upon English interference with American rights, as far back as the reign of George the Third, the principle of the opposition whereto by the Colonies, he has pirated and emblazoned on his flag.

It has taken me by surprise to see Mr. Douglas seek refuge under the influence of the opinion of the Supreme Court of the United States, in the Dred Scott case. He must be very easily satisfied with the smallest quota of consolation. A timid man would shun the precincts of a tribunal whose dictum is the ruin of his cause. Not so, Mr. Douglas. He enters with the air of one who has got the ear of the Court: but his confidence is assumed, for after lingering awhile, he becomes chilled, and is repulsed by the gloom of the severe tribunal. The doctrine of Popular Sovereignty finds no favor in the *Opinion*, but a different result, and one which he bitterly deprecates, looms up like a spectre to appal him. Mr. Douglas and the Supreme Court occupy one position in common—they plant themselves equally, as to the power of the Federal Government to acquire territory outside of the original limits of the United States, and the power of instituting temporary governments for such acquired territory necessarily consequent upon its acquisition, upon the same Constitutional provision, viz: "New States may be admitted by Congress into this Union,"—this they jointly say is the only authority to acquire and to govern. But agreeing in the premise, they widely differ in its results on the slavery question. Mr. Douglas affirms "Popular Sovereignty is the legitimate offspring in the Territories," of this right to acquire and to govern—with a terminus attached to it, thus, "the Constitution of the United States neither establishes nor prohibits Slavery in the Territories, beyond the power of the people legally to control it; but (it) leaves the people thereof perfectly free to form and regulate their domestic institutions, (slavery) in their own way, subject only to the Constitution of the United States." Here is the goal of Mr. Douglas' reasoning. Not so, but far different the dictum of the Court. In a series of professional inference and in language, clear and free from all vulgar redundancy, the Supreme Court proceeds step by step, from the same Constitutional provision, to show, first, the inevitable consequence of that provision, as to the right of the Federal Government to acquire territory, then, the power to preserve it, being the necessary consequence of acquisition, and to apply it to the purposes for which it was acquired; next the right to institute temporary governments therefor, and then in more minute recital and detail, the powers and restrictions of these Territorial Governments, and the rights of persons and property therein. Let me not be understood as yielding any unfair preference to the reasoning of the Supreme Court over that of Mr. Douglas; far from it—I hold an equal balance, although I confess to a leaning towards dignity in language. The Court have not, of course, combined their reasoning on the slavery question in the Territories, into an extract, with a title in two words endorsed on it, ready to distribute out gratis as a panacea for the political ills of the country; but, like able jurists, well versed in the doctrine of construction, and warping, thereby, the plain intent and spirit of the Constitution, the canker vice inherent in all ages in the Interpreters of law, they lead to the conclusion, among other things, "that the government and the citizen both entering a Territory under the authority of the Constitution, with their respective rights defined and marked out, and the property of a citizen being protected by the Constitution, if that property be a slave (which, by the Constitution, is recognized as such,) no legislation of Congress, or of the Territorial Government, its creature, nor consequently of the people of a Territory who elect the Legislature, can exercise any power over such slave property, beyond what the Constitution confers, nor lawfully deny any right which it has reserved"—to meet this result, it is idle to say that Slavery is subject to the local law, like all other property of the citizen, as Mr. Douglas would fain make us consider it; for there is no local law, all the law in a Territory is Congressional—in other words, the Congressional is the local law. Here there is an open rupture, with defiance

to the doctrine of Popular Sovereignty. Mr. Douglas deprecates it, and insists that this cannot be the true construction of
the *Opinion*, and that the Court means something else, for he
seems to consider the *Opinion* as oracular, and that undertaking
to interpret the true meaning of the Constitution, it stands
itself in need of a high priest to discover its own import.   If
the Slavery question be included among the forbidden powers,
that is cannot be reached or affected in any way in the Territories by any legislation, Congressional or Territorial, but is
there carried and preserved, like all other property, sacred by
force of the Constitution, then Mr. Douglas is in despair ; for
the authority that brings and guards it so sacredly in the
Territories, exercises the same kind offices towards Slavery in
the States, and Pennsylvania and Illinois are no more
exempt from the institution Constitutionally, than Kansas or
Utah.   And such is the meaning of the oracle as interpreted
by another authority, the chief Executive of the Nation, who
announces that the Supreme Court decides that Slavery "exists
in Kansas by virtue of the Constitution of the United States,
and that Kansas is, therefore, at this moment, as much a Slave
State as Georgia or South Carolina,"—to which interpretation
Mr. Douglas responds in despair, "Why does it not exist in
Pennsylvania by virtue of the same Constitution?"

Mr. Douglas and the Supreme Court do not then agree as to
the legal condition of Slavery in the Territories. Starting
from the same centre, they reach different points of the
circumference. There must be something radically wrong in
their primary position, else sensible men like the Senator, and
sensible and learned men like the Court, could not have
wandered away so far from each other and from the truth.
They have mistaken the Constitution. Hence the fanciful
folly of this doctrine of "Popular Sovereignty"—an insult to
the high intelligence of the country, although an invention
worthy of the erratic genius of its author. Hence, also, the
commentary on slavery by the Supreme Court—a monstrous
product, making evil no longer partial but universal, and
justifying the commission of political felony throughout the
land, in the name of a benign Constitution.

The Constitution of the United States, notwithstanding its
novelty as an institute, and the vast influence that it brings to
bear upon the subject matters of which it treats, being the
most important that interest mankind either for good or evil,
is nothing but a law, and, notwithstanding its vital authority
and scope, contains within itself no element of creative power
beyond the simplest act of legislation. A State statute,

erecting a turnpike in Missouri, or a municipal corporation in
Ohio, is obscure legislation, yet it possesses the same kindred
germ of authority that is inherent in the Constitution. On
the other hand, the potent Constitution is limited by the same
natural inability that confines the insignficant statute. When
the act of the Legislature grants the turnpike right, or the
corporation privilege, it defines and limits the right or the
privilege, but it does not assume a power beyond its sphere,
and create or bestow the locality of the city or the road.
These things are *in esse*, provided beforehand by a power
different from the legislative, and belonging to another order
of acquisition altogether—they are of the matters which
legislation may act upon, but cannot confer. The Constitution
having adjusted with wondrous comprehension and brevity,
several powers on the subject matters entitled to priority,
addresses itself, in the third section of its fourth Article, to
ascertain and define what powers it will entrust to its agent,
Congress, in regard, first, to the admission of new States into
the Union, and secondly, to the disposing of and making all
needful rules and regulations respecting the territory or other
property *belonging* to the United States. It does not confer
the soil, the material substance out of which the new States
are to be carved, nor the territory, the disposal of which, and
the making of all needful rules and regulations respecting
which, it grants to Congress, for this the Constitutional provision
itself distinctly declares *belongs* to the United States—*belongs*
to the United States either *in esse* or in *futuro*, and whenever
so *belonging*, to come *instanter* under the operation of the law
of the Constitution—that law applicable to the Territory which.
belonged to the Federal Government when the Constitution
was adopted, as, for instance, the gift of Virginia in 1784, and
applicable in all future time to all other territory acquired by
the United States by virtue of the right inherent in every
sovereignty, viz: Gift, purchase, or conquest. The acquisition
of territory is an inherent right in a Nation, not conferred by
constitutional law; so penetrating is this truth, that one
instance will suffice, which I shall put in the form interrogata-
tive: Did the Constitution of the United States confer on the
Nation the soil of the thirteen Colonies, or did the Nation
acquire it by conquest from Great Britain, independent
altogether of a Constitution, not then existence? When the
land was acquired, it was first partitioned into States; this
was one disposition made of it, independent of the Constitution.
Again, the Nation altered its political *status* and adopted a
new rule called the Constitution, for the government of the

country. To require of the framers of that Constitution to grant therein, to the Nation, the right of the acquisition of territory, upon which the Constitution was to operate, is a demand of that which it was not in the power of the conscript fathers to bestow. They knew their sphere and they kept it. Theirs was the wisdom to elaborate a system of good government for the territory, belonging to the Nation, without vainly usurping a power that was not theirs to exercise. Hence the language of the provision is singularly free from any such usurpation. If the power to acquire territory for the creation of new States, to be disposed of and ruled in its embryo condition in a certain way, was intended to be conferred upon the Nation by the framers of the Constitution, a proposition that would stultify their intelligence, why is there not eviscerated by construction from the same Constitutional provision, the gift to the Nation of the power to acquire other property, such as ships of war, arsenals, &c.? Is it an inherent right in the Nation to acquire such property as this, and yet does it require a Constitutional provision to authorize the acquisition of territory—does the Constitution draw such a distinction in national property? Congress is empowered "to exercise exclusive legislation, in all cases whatever, over all places purchased by the Legislature of the State in which the same shall be, for the erection of forts, magazines, arsenals, dock yards, and other needful buildings;" thus when territory is needed for federal purposes in a State, since there the General Government has no inherent right of the acquisition of land, being a component part of the whole, with rights reserved, the Constitution confers upon Congress the power of purchase and exclusive jurisdiction, not constructively, but in explicit language, altogether distinct form the total silence in regard to the acquisition of territory, outside the original limits of the United States. If the Constitution speaks out in regard to the acquisition of a dock yard by the Federal Government, and the exercise of jurisdiction therein, a matter comparatively insignificant and temporary, and yet obtaining a positive provision, although the territory lay within the precincts of one of the component parts of the Federal Sovereignty, how much more explicit and elaborate, beyond the reach of tortuous construction or fallible inference, would not the framers of the Constitution have pointed out and defined, if they conceived they possessed the power, how territory outside the original limits of the United States was to be acquired by the Federal Government, whether by gift, by purchase, (as in the cases of Arsenal sites,) or by conquest

—especially when such territory was destined for the most exalted purposes, not the erection of forts, magazines, arsenals and dockyards, but the erection of empires, co-ordinate with the original States, and sweeping, when launched, into line with them under the shadow of the mighty banner of the Constitution—such transcendent interests would not be over-looked, nor slightly touched upon, much less exposed, as the subject matter of speculative philosophy of old was to conjecture, to the tender mercies of judicial or political construction. The right of the acquisition of territory then being a right inherent in the sovereignty, and outside the sphere of the Constitution, does not flow, as Mr. Douglas and the Supreme Court infer by construction, from the power expressly granted to Congress to admit new States into the Union, and hence the Senator and the Court have mistaken the Constitution.

The acquisition of territory is a right inherent in every sovereignty, which sovereignty, unless limited by Constitu-tional provision, is absolute over every matter subject to legislation in the territory when acquired—sovereignty cannot be parcelled out, distributed, or confined otherwise than by original compact—if there is no limit or restraint imposed upon it, it is absolute in itself, and to subtract from its absolute nature, you must show the authority. When the Federal Government acquires a territory, its power therein, over every subject matter, Slavery included, is supreme, unless confined and limited by the Constitution of the United States. Let us inspect the Constitution, then, and examine its provisions, what of them are, upon the subject of Slavery in the Terri-tories: the relation of Master and Slave is extracted from the third subdivision of the second section of the fourth article of the Constitution, thus : "No person, held to service or labor in one State, under the Laws thereof, escaping into another, shall, in consequence of any law or regulation therein, be discharged from such service or labor, but shall be delivered up, on claim of the party to whom such service or labor may be due;" herein is the only provision made by the Constitution in regard to Slavery in the United States, and the cautious, nay, tender use of terms patent in its language, manifests distinctly the reluctant spirit of the humane men, who, by compulsion, drafted and adopted it. What Mr. Douglas and the Supreme Court coarsely term Slavery, the Constitution, with the regard due to fallen humanity, denominates service or labor, a different grade of descent altogether, let the gentlemen know, from the bathos of Slavery—and they, who, with equal accuracy, are degraded by the titles of Slave and Master, (as much a degradation to the one as to the other,) are properly named therein, by natural transposition, a servant or laborer, a party claimant or creditor. I feel for the indignities offered by the powerful to the weak—they excite emotions I cannot control—"Names," exclaims the Senator, "often deceive persons in respect to the nature and substance of things"—he could have employed far more appropriate language than this for his purpose, where he uses it, but it suits me here exactly, and I claim it without compliment, although it is very probably the only claim I shall ever make upon the wisdom of the Senator—if there be anything in the quotation, I stamp, by virtue thereof, the charge of deception upon Mr. Douglas and the Supreme Court, in that they have used "names which deceive persons in respect to the nature and substance of things," and to make it the more poignant to the gentleman, I employ, with the utmost propriety, his own language as the sentence of his condemnation. The solemn periods of statesmanship and of the august Tribunal of Law of the last resort, should not be contaminated with the professional epithet of the slave-dealer—there should be no bias, for there should be no feeling—no bias of language, as well as no bias of its spirit and import, lest the use of the wrong term should lead, as it invariably does, to the wrong interpretation. When the chief agents of the Constitution, it seems, intend to admeasure out its spirit unfairly, like petty dealers, they have recourse to the use of fraudulent weights and measures.

No portion of the Constitution, save this veiled and guarded provision, seeks apology at the hands of mankind—elsewhere the genius of the great law rules firmly over its vast confines, and speaks of the interests confided to his charge in language not to be misunderstood ; here alone his air is deprecatory and his tongue falters, for he was called upon to make a sacrifice of human right at the passionate pleading of his fair and favorite twin daughter of the South, and he was forced by affection for the fond minion to yield—doubtless she was entitled to every other indulgence save this—independent of her native charms, the rich and magnificent scenery of her abode, the lavish wealth that surrounded her in Orient profusion, she could point to the heroic deeds of her sons emblazoned on the fields of carnage and the page of history— she was entitled to every consideration in the gift of the Constitution; alas! that she was so beloved and deserving as to entreat and obtain a boon, which being violative of human right, has been injurious to none other's welfare more than to her own.

But call the thing itself labor or slavery, and call the person owing it a laborer or a slave, immaterial as to the question of the power of the legal disposition of the subject in the Territories—Mr. Douglas quotes the Supreme Court to the effect, that from the clause which provides for the rendition of fugitive slaves "the right of property in slaves is distinctly and expressly affirmed in the Constitution"—and coinciding with the Opinion herein, he proceeds further, and points out what class of persons the provision explicitly states shall be deemed slaves, viz: the persons held to service or labor in a State *under the laws thereof*—not satisfied with this position, however, he extends the limit of his term, and avers that State means Territory also, proving by various references to the Constitution, to Mr. Jefferson and Mr. Madison, that the word was indiscriminately applied to a State or Territory— the extension of the term's import, however, cannot avail him; the Supreme Court were as well aware of the meaning of those words of limitation *"under the laws thereof"* as Mr. Douglas, and could strain a State into a Territory with as much facility, but they avoided the fatal passage in silence, for they knew its bearing. One word, by way of preliminary, however—the use of redundant epithet or adverb is always proof of weakness or conciousness—when a man wants to convince another of the truth of that which is repugnant to him, he is liberal of language in the same proportion as he is needy of fact, and interlards the use of it with superlatives and impiety—the language of truth, on the contrary, is simple and shuns expletives. Now, "the right of property in slaves is *not* distinctly and expressly affirmed in the Constitution," as the Supreme Court, with such ambitious confidence and redundancy, assert : on the contrary, if the right of property in the person, in contradistinction to the right of property in the labor or service which the person owes, is to be found there at all, it is inferentially stated, and not distinctly and expressly. But Mr. Douglas, who harps in so cheerily always with the Supreme Court, whenever they make a forced or unfaithful exposition, as usual with that class that drove Timon to misanthropy, excels even the tautology of a Court of Chancery.

"A slave," says Mr. Douglas, "is a person held to service or labor in a State *under the laws thereof*"—and further "the word 'States' is used in the clause providing for the rendition of fugitive slaves, applicable to all political communities under the authority of the United States, including the Territories, as well as the several States of the Union"—therefore, Mr.

Douglas' full definition of a slave is "a person held to service
or labor in a State or Territory, *under the laws thereof*"—this
would appear to be conclusive, and of all men, should most
satisfy the Senator himself—a person may owe service or labor
in a State or Territory, to another and not be a slave—it
requires the vivifying power of Law ordained by the Legislative authority of a State or Territory to transmute the debt of
service or labor into slavery, and the person held to such
service or labor into a slave—but he may owe service or labor
to another in a State, and the laws thereof not only not hold
him to it, thereby leaving him, as it were, negatively free, but
it may positively enact that there shall be neither slavery nor
slave for service or labor due in the State or Territory—this is altogether independent of the Constitutional clause, authorizing
the recovery of a fugitive from labor, and shows the forced and
unnatural construction of Mr. Douglas and the Supreme Court
of the provision, as to the amount of recognition given by
the Constitution to what they call slavery—the unbiassed
import of the clause at most is, that the Federal Government,
not intermeddling itself with slavery in any way, in its own
capacity, shall effect for the citizen of a State, and as Mr.
Douglas adds, a Territory, where slavery exists under its laws,
the recovery of a fugitive from labor, because without this
interference, it would not be within the power of the citizen of
the State to make such a recovery, without a violation of the
Local Law of the State where the refugee escaped—this is
the very limited foundation of the vast superstructure, which
has been piled upon it so lavishly, that the Constitutional
basis can no longer be traced beneath the architectural order
of the Goths—the provision merely recognizes a fact that
existed at the time of its passage, and which may further
exist in a future State or Territory, as the laws thereof may
enact, namely the holding of a person to service or labor in a
State by force of its Local Law, and declaring that such person
escaping into another State where such law did not exist, but,
perhaps, one the very opposite, shall not be discharged in
consequence of the law or regulation of the State to which he
escapes, but be delivered up, on claim of the party to whom
such service or labor may be due—nor is it herein so apparent
by what process or proceeding the delivery is to be effected.
The Supreme Court, I presume, (for I, too, have claim upon
presumption,) will admit that the Law is Penal—in the spirit
and terms in which it is interpreted by them and Mr. Douglas.
Slave and Slavery for Laborer and Service, the conversion of
a person, whom comparative anatomy may dissect, and find as

physically finished (independent of the master mind,) by the mould of the Hand of the Almighty, as the subject body of a Chief Justice, into a chattle, a bureau, or an ambling mule, it is believed by the honest masses to be inhumanely Penal— it is not entitled then to any facilities either of construction or enforcement—if the provision be impotent and lame from malformation, and the remedy of the prohibited wrong beyond reach from uncertainty, it does not become a christian Congress, Court and Senator to pretend to the gift of miracles irreligiously, and assume to make the blind see and the lame walk— the age of miracles with some of them at least is past—Mr. Douglas has pretensions, but I have no confidence in his ever working a miracle—there is nothing in the provision that exclusively or by priority requires the Federal Government, its Legislature, or officers to be the medium or agents of the delivery—the sentence is barren of instruction thuswise, either affirmatively or by the Court's favorite process of inference—its silence surprises, and means all it does not say— if asked, how can you enforce the provision except by Congressional action and the agency thereby created, in the cause of humanity, I repulse the interrogatory as insolent, and will not furnish the aggressor with any weapon of offense—if I wrest from his hand, which I now haughtily do, the sword of the executioner, unjustifiably furnished him by Act of Congress, it is enough for me so to disarm him—I am not called upon to cull from the brilliant armory of the Constitution the bloody weapon of the brigand—it is not there.

I am, in politeness, here required to apologize to Mr. Douglas for unintentional neglect, arising from a division of favors, which I did not propose at the outset, between him and the Supreme Court—I shall devote myself, therefore, more exclusively to the gentleman henceforth to the end, and here cast off from me the Tribunal—not that I do not part from these judges with regret, and they may some day obtain from me the sole and strict attention to which they are eminently entitled—but I am now engaged and interested in Mr. Douglas, and shall not be tempted to quit the pleasant pursuit, even for the golden prize that surely awaits the explorer, after he has demolished this Judicial Fabric and searched its ruins.

I admit I have toyed with the Senator in the Barrier in which he has placed himself—secure of him, I have paused and taken rest—Tamerlane inhumanly constructed an Iron Cage in which he immured and exhibited his victim—but he was a Pagan and a tyrant, and no example whatever for an American gentleman—I weave no meshes either of cob-web or of iron—Mr. Douglas' tissue is of his own formation, and encloses him as artistically as a spider's woof, and as inexorably as ribs of steel—" A slave is a person held to service or labor in a State or Territory, *under the laws thereof"*—Territorial laws which must be conformatory to the Constitution, are the only ones in force in the Territory, and can be enacted only by Congress or its Deputy, the Territorial Legislature, elected as Congress provides—if the Territorial law holds a person to service or labor, and thereby makes him a slave, the transmutation is the act of Congress, the agent of the Constitution, or if the Territorial law does not hold a person to service or labor, and is silent thereon, thereby negatively refusing to make a person owing service or labor a slave, or, if it positively declares that such person shall be nevertheless free, it is equally the act of Congress, the agent of the Constitution; that can pass no law or do no act without the authority of its principal—Territorial, like State law, can thus establish or prohibit slavery in the Territory at will—such, now, is Mr. Douglas on slavery in the Territories; collate herewith his pronunciamento to his followers and the Nation, " The Constitution of the United States neither establishes nor prohibits slavery in the States or Territories beyond the power of the people legally to control it, but leaves the people thereof perfectly free to form and regulate their domestic institutions in their own way, subject only to the Constitution of the United States"—when Congress deputes its legislative power to a Territorial Legislature, it elects its deputy by the vote of the people—but the act of the lawful agent is the act of his principal, and the law of the Territorial Legislature, either establishing or prohibiting slavery, is the law of Congress authorized by the Constitution. Let Mr. Douglas suit himself —if a slave is a person held to service or labor in a Territory under the laws thereof, the Constitution of the United States does establish or prohibit slavery in the Territory at will, beyond all other power, and through the agencies, which it must necessarily employ, either Congress, or its deputy, the Territorial Legislature, elected as Congress provides, and Congress is not limited to any form of deputy or mode of election—that is discretionary—and if the laws of a Territory establish or prohibit slavery at will, these laws being the act of Congress, slavery is thus established or prohibited in the Territory by the Constitution. The subtle drift of Mr. Douglas that when Congress deputes its authority to the Territorial Legislature, in whole or in part, the Legislature is elected by the people, who may thereby be said to have the power to establish or prohibit slavery at will, shall not avail him, for it smells rank to heaven of the Legerdemain which is called Little, without the huge Adfix. The will of the people here is the will of Congress and the Constitution, selected by the master powers on account of its exact reflex and similitude, and totally absorbed and unknown when the result is reached—it cuts back to its authors and is its authors' act. So much for the counterfeit casuistry that would not pass current even in the schools. If the Senator, then, be correct in his statement (for, be it observed, I make none of my own, but studiously keep aloof from any contact with him whatever,) that a slave is "a person held to service or labor in a Territory, *under the laws thereof,*" he assumes the office of the Lictor, and precipitates his own pronunciamento headlong from the Tarpeian Rock of the Constitution—and worse still, he commits in addition the crime of parricide, without the merit of a Roman Sacrifice for the good of his country, for the malefactor whom he immolates is his own illegitimate offspring.

In support of his Doctrine of Popular Sovereignty Mr. Douglas cites the Act of Congress of 1850, called the Compromise Measures, the resolutions of political parties, Whig and Democratic, assembled in National Convention in 1852 for the nomination of candidates for the offices of President and Vice President, adopting and affirming the principle of these Compromise Measures on the question of slavery in the organization of Territorial Governments and the admission of new States, the Kansas-Nebraska Act, of 1854, based on the principle of the Compromise Measures, so far as they are applicable to territorial organizations, the unanimous vote of the Delegates of the Democratic party from every State in the Union, in National Convention assembled in 1856, recognising and adopting the principles contained in the Organic Laws establishing the Territories of Kansas and Nebraska, and the letter of Mr. Buchanan, the nominee of this Convention, approving the recent legislation of Congress respecting domestic slavery—the principle involved in these multitudinous citations, as far as they refer to the organization of Territories is, *that the people of the Territories should decide the slavery question for themselves through the action of their Territorial Legislature.* Much stress is laid upon the promise of peace to the country, made in the speeches of Senators, the resolutions and reports of Conventions and their committees, and the affirmatory letter of the present Chief Magistrate, by the adoption of this precept. Let us select a few of these consolations : "The wisdom of those measures is attested, not less

31

by their salutary and beneficial effects in allaying sectional
agitation and restoring peace and harmony to an irritated and
distracted people, than by the cordial and almost universal
approbation with which they have been received and sanctioned
by the whole country"—"by the uniform application of the
Democratic principle of non-intervention by Congress with
slavery in State or Territory, or in the District of Columbia, to
the organization of Territories, and to the admission of new
States, with or without domestic slavery as they may elect,
the equal rights of all will be preserved intact, the original
compacts of the Constitution maintained inviolate, and the
perpetuity and expansion of this Union insured to its utmost
capacity of embracing in peace and harmony any future
American State that may be constituted or annexed with a
Republican form of Government"—"the recent legislation of
Congress," reads Mr. Buchanan's letter, "respecting domestic
slavery, derived, as it has been, from the original and pure
fountain of legitimate political power, the will of the majority,
promises, ere long, to allay the dangerous excitement—this
legislation is founded upon principles as ancient as free
government itself, and in accordance with them has simply
declared that the people of a Territory, like those of a State,
*shall decide for themselves whether slavery shall or shall not exist
within their limits.*

Upon these and similar promises of good result to the peace
and welfare of the country, Mr. Douglas relies for proof of
the efficacy of the Doctrine of Popular Soveriegnty—they
differ however somewhat from the certificates that usually announce the virtue of other specifics, these being always furnished by patients or their friends, after they have tested the
truth of the cure, and have been wholly, or in part restored
thereby, whereas the endorsements of the infallible compound
of Popular Sovereignty, are purely prophetic, and these good
friends of the patient public, Senators, Conventions and
Presidents, generously subscribe the flaming certificate before
the medicine is tested—how if the facts nullify the promises,
and convert the Patriot Douglas into a very Cassandra, whose
vaticinations by the decree of heaven, must never be credited—
have the Compromise Measures of 1850, has the Kansas
Nebraska Act of 1854, the resolutions of National Conventions, and the endorsement of a Presidential Candidate meta-
morphosed a policy into a principle, an expediency into a
right, or the non-intervention by Congress with slavery in a
Territory, or the District of Columbia, into the want of the
Constitutional power of such intervention? have they con-

vinced us that the Constitution does not authorize its agent, Congress, to decide whether slavery shall or shall not exist within the limits of a Territory, where no other Legislative power lives or can live, by virtue of the Constitution, except the Legislative power of Congress exercised either *per se* or authoritatively *per alium?* have they convinced us that there can be two Legislative Organizations in a Territory, the one Constitutional and Congressional, to act upon every topic of Legislation, save slavery, and the other, a Popular Sovereignty Legislature, of which the framers of the Constitution never dreamed to ascertain and enact the wishes of the people of the Territory on the question of slavery alone? have they convinced us that salutary and beneficial effects in allaying sectional agitation and restoring peace and harmony to an irritated and distracted people, have followed from the wisdom of those measures, when the blood of Kansas, (the nursling of one of those Acts that carried healing on its wings,) still runs in the memory of man as deeply as when it fell in torrents on her soil, or when, still worse, the Senator, who fain would claim the whole paternity of the monstrous doctrine to himself, and allow to others no share in its procreation, unlike the fœtid gift of the Gods to their poor and barren host, has, since the passage of these Acts, up to the present hour, made sectional agitation, irritation and distraction, on the slavery question, a profession, which he practises unweariedly on the most liberal terms, a contingent fee? What affinity exists between the vigorous and lusty Constitution, and such hermaphrodite legislation, Conventions and Statesmen? Is there no blush on the face of vulgar ambition that it should parade before the Nation this morbid rhetoric, a painted and spangled garb, such as is studiously worn by the diviner to impress his audience with the belief of his familiarity with fortune? The philosophic Statesman, when he beholds good result notwithstanding the abeyance of principle, sits silent if not satisfied, and pleased with the benefit accruing to his country, ruminates calmly on the occasion of the ripe harvest which she reaps and he did not sow ; but what manner of man is that, philosophic Statesman or bad citizen, who forebodes peace when it is war, general harmony when it is sectional agitation, universal approbation when it is irritation and distraction everywhere, equal rights, original compacts, perpetuity and expansion, when it is a jumble and a chaos, into which the Constitutional system is cast by these raw apprentices, who vainly struggle to reunite the fragments they have disjointed, and call, each his patch work, the old Constitution. I care not whether they be Gods or men in the form of Presidents or Conventions, who rob the Constitution of its Territorial rights; I care not for the imposing pretense of grandiloquent publication, when it embodies no fact and testifies to no truth; I abjure the technical silence that would make believe, that the Compromise Measures of 1850 and the Kansas-Nebraska Act of 1854 met no soldierly opposition from stern veterans of the Constitution, the old and immortal guard, or the inuendo that every member of these Democratic Conventions was, by birthright, a statesman, according to the Constitutional standard, because he applauded these acts of political harlotry openly committed in the day of the loss of public virtue; these things have no weight or influence with me, when I plant the ordinance of 1787 drafted under the eye if not by the pen of Mr. Jefferson, (although it is said by Mr. Douglas, with his usual manliness, that it was passed by the remnant of the Congress of the Confederation, in New York, after its most eminent members had gone to Philadelphia,) against the opinion of the Supreme Court denying its Constitutionality, and the Missouri Compromise Act of 1820 against the Douglas Act of 1854 which repeals it. The Ordinance of 1787 is the twin brother of the Constitution, born in the same year, of the same august parentage, with Mr. Jefferson and Mr. Madison the same sponsors for both, and however differing in proportion, as members of a family will, belonging to the same pure republican stock of legislation ; the Compromise Act of 1820 lived a blameless and quiet life of public utility for thirty-four years, during which every virtue that was originally claimed for it was realized. The harbinger of calm, it more than performed its promise—imbued with the spirit of the Constitution, it breathed peace and induced repose—not only North of its line, 36°30′, where it ruled supreme, did sectional feeling abate, and the fell spirit of slavery strife die out, but even South thereof, where its jurisdiction was joint, such was the genial and lenient nature of the law, no controversy arose on the partnership account—but Mr. Douglas' Constitutional slumbers were disturbed by its existence on the statute book, and the tender conscience of Mr. Cass was sorely troubled with doubts of its legitimacy; hear the elderly Secretary, then Senator, "I have already stated my belief that the rightful power of internal legislation in the Territories belongs to the people"—another votary in these hopeful times of a double headed Legislature in the Territories. This blow at the Missouri Compromse, first given by letter in 1848, to cultivate and seduce sectional support for the Presidency, cost the gentleman dearly, and he had the right to remember the law with a vengeance—he did, and voted successfully with Mr. Douglas to repeal it, the wisest and most beneficent act of legislation ever passed by Congress, before which the Tariff and Bank questions pale and shrink, in reference to the internal peace and repose of the country—but it shall revive, summoned from its cerements into a new existence by the potent call of the Constitution. Mr. Douglas places the utmost reliance upon the action of Senators and Conventions and Presidential candidates—the Missouri Compromise Act relies solely on the self-interest of a multitudinous people, who will be no longer disturbed by Mr. Douglas' never ending slavery agitation, and the miserable ambition that begets it—when the elements are ripe, the lightning flashes to restore nature's equipoise—objects either elevated or low, Senators or negroes, melt before its transit—the indignation of the American people, when deceived, is not as potent as the dread artillery of heaven, but it executes swift vengeance for all human purposes, whilst the thunder of their voice rumbles fearfully along the hills and elevations of power, as it purges the political atmosphere.

Were it asked of a dispassionate and intelligent citizen, whose judgment was not warped by any personal purpose, other than what is common to him with every individual member of the Nation, "read me these three clauses of the 3rd and 2nd Sections of the 4th Article of the Constitution, and expound to me their true import, viz: Sec. 3rd, clause 1st: ' New States may be admitted by the Congress into this Union; but no New State shall be formed or erected within the jurisdiction of any other State, without the consent of the Legislatures of the States concerned, as well as of the Congress'—2nd, 'The Congress shall have power to dispose of and make all needful Rules and Regulations respecting the Territory or other property belonging to the United States, and nothing in this Constitution shall be so construed as to prejudice any claims of the United States or of any particular State'—Sec. 2nd, clause 3rd, 'No person held to service or labor in one State under the laws thereof, escaping into another, shall in consequence of any Law or Regulation therein, be discharged from such service or labor, but shall be delivered up, on claim of the party to whom such service or labor may be due;'" such a citizen may truly answer, in terms somewhat similar hereto. "When the power of the admission by Congress of new States into the Union was authorized by the Constitution, the only territory belonging to the Federal Government was that ceded by Virginia in 1784, called the North West Terri-

the matter at all, except by means of the Territorial Legislature, which Congress under the Constitution authorizes them to elect—what species of political Legerdemain is this? Does the gentleman consider the national intellect idiotic, and that we have lost all reverence for the founders of the true doctrine of Popular Sovereignty, to allow him thus to pilfer our birthright, and plunder and defile their wisdom? Does he rank himself beside the colossal proportions of Thomas Jefferson? Does he announce to this Nation that he has discovered what Jefferson lost? Very well, I proclaim, although it is amiable in Mr. Douglas to put inferentially Mr. Jefferson as a subaltern to himself, that such is my weakness, in accordance with the divine delicacy of the import of the classic lines (I implore the pardon of the Senator,) I would rather seem wrong with Mr. Jefferson than be right with Mr. Douglas.

I have done. In the adopted State of the Senator, among other gifts conferred on her liberally by the hand of a genial nature, is a stream, either branch of which is lovely enough to adapt itself to my present purpose—so placid is its bosom, that the ingenuous youth of the country can safely float upon it in his tiny cock-boat, lingering around its islets. or drifting sportively along its fragrant banks—let the gentleman beware —the calm stream becomes occasionally, from cause, a heady and an angry current, rupturing those banks, and spreading into a wide waste of waters, to cross which in the leaky skiff that Mr. Douglas paddles, would be perilous—I warn him of his safety.

ERRATUM.—In the dedication of this pamphlet, the word " received," in the 5th line, should read *revived*.

terms "Popular Sovereignty," and the conclusion that men's minds would naturally run to, that, as it was insisted upon so strenuously by the Senator for the first time, it had no previous existence in either the theory or practise of the Government —this *ruse* has had its day—the self-complacency with which the gentleman has formerly stroked his chin at the ephemeral success of his project, has given way to the alarm that always follows the discovery of a little petty plot. The doctrine of Popular Sovereignty is the very germ of the Constitution, and the noble offspring of its founders and defenders, from the first hour of its existence to the present, and Mr. Douglas is as much entitled to any special part in the great principle, as a pirate is to a portion of the cargo he feloniously plunders, or to the inspiration of the author whose volume he publishes as his own—he not only robs the Constitution and the uniform line of Congressional action for upwards of half a century, of the doctrine, but the moment he gets it into his grasp, he emasculates it. Popular Sovereignty in the Territories was always exercised in its full proportions, manly and exalted as they are, until of late when Mr. Douglas takes hold of the magazine, and peddles out the principle in broken doses. When Congressional action was heretofore applied to a Territory, the voice of the Nation at large was heard on the subject, and every interest was consulted and defended—the pro-slavery interest especially, for that by the Constitution, the white man who owned a hundred negroes had sixty-one voices in Congress, whilst the white man who owned no negroes had only one— the slave owner, therefore, could not complain of his interest being neglected, when the national will, on the pure principle of Popular Sovereignty, was consulted and expressed in Congress, in legislating for the Territory—but beyond this, the uniform rule of that legislation from the admission of Kentucky in 1792 to the late auspicious times of Senator Calhoun and Douglas, was to confer upon the people of the Territories the right to elect their own Legislature, and thus secure a true representation of the will of the majority as to local or general interests—does the Senator want a better Popular Sovereignty Doctrine than this, being the doctrine of the founders? It appears he does, and let us see what it is : he vehemently exclaims, exclude the question of slavery in the Territories out of Congress, where the will of the people, the entire Nation, to whom the Territory belongs, can be alone heard, on the true principle of Popular Sovereignty, and let the people of the Territory settle the question for themselves, when they have no power under heaven to do so, or to touch granted, in legal form, her Southwest territory to the shores of the Pacific—it is apparent herefrom what anticipations as to the admission of new States into the Union, the framers of the Constitution entertained—let us remember that what Virginia had already ceded in the Northwest, and what might be expected for similar cession in the Southwest, was a species of *terra incognita*, that the adventurous spirit of our people was comparatively unknown, and that the impetus which freedom gives a nation, to ascertain and vindicate its territorial rights, had, as yet, no scope of time to exert itself. The Constitution, then, embodied in this provision cases that have never yet occurred, and the assertion may be fairly ventured, that they never contemplated, as a body, the admission of new States by Congress into the Union out of any other territory than what then belonged to the original thirteen States—hence the reason why States or Territories are indiscriminately termed States, because they were or were of States. The purchase of Louisiana was not yet anticipated, nor the annexation of Texas, nor the conquest of Utah and California—Cuba was not yet yearned after—coupled with these impressive reasons, founded on surrounding facts, and apparent in the Constitutional language itself, the transitory existence of a Territory, to-day, a wilderness, to-morrow, the abode of the adventurous citizen, drawing to him, by the attractions of a virgin soil and a novel life, the very acme to many of the existence of a freeman, in a few years crowds of daring men, until their number reached the Congressional climax, when by natural and brief process this chrysalis condition was changed into the full grown existence of State life, the Constitution did not then define, nor was it needed to define with the same accuracy or scope of provision a political condition, that was normal and transient, which it was both needful and provident, it should with unerring care and in distinct language, adopt for a new State and a new Federal government, that was finally settled and was meant to be perpetual—hence, the limited and guarded sovereignty granted to the Federal Government by the Constitution over the States that were and the States that were to be, the law defining, with rigid accuracy, positively and negatively, how far that sovereignty was to reach and where it was to cease— hence, too, the reservation to the States and the people of all the rights not granted to the Federal Government—and hence, also, the unlimited sovereign power, inherent in the General Government over the Territory, is untouched by any other restriction, if restriction it may be termed, and that

tory, a tract of country North-west of the River Ohio, indifferently defined as to boundary, and a wilderness occupied by
the savage Indian, with very sparse exceptions—undoubtedly
it was anticipated, that as Virginia had ceded, so in like
manner other States of the Union that owned surplus territory,
with only nominal or fictitious possession of it, would follow
her example and relinquish to the United States their
Sovereignty therein—this is apparent from the further provision in the same clause of the section, declaring that no new
States shall be formed or erected within the jurisdiction of any
other State, nor any State be formed by the junction of two
or more States or parts of States, without the consent of the
Legislatures of the States concerned, as well as of the Congress,
being the mode adopted in the case of the Virginia cession,
which was first passed by her Legislature, afterwards accepted
and ordered to be recorded and enrolled among the Acts of
the United States in Congress assembled—it is memorable
here, however, that not a word is uttered as to the acquisition
of Territory outside the limits of the United States, either
populous or waste, filled with cities or with forests, that being
a right inherent in the Nation—other things are also apparent
from the language of this provision—that, for instance two
States or parts of two States may be ceded as Territory to the
General Government, for the reason in the first case, that the
citizens of two small States may consider their condition
would be benefited by a mutual union of both into one State
of ample proportions, by the Constitutional process of first, a
Territorial, next a new State existence, and in the second, for
the reason that two States may consider, that each having a
tract of country belonging to it, a profitless surplusage to
itself, and too small for a State purpose, but each lying contiguous
to the other, and furnishing sufficient dimensions for a State,
may be patriotically ceded to the United States, on the Virginia
plan—no instance of a cession in the first mentioned case ever
occurred, State pride very probably forbidding the merging
of one State into another, under any circumstances, or even
relinquishing a small tract of country, though excessive, as
many of them could, for territorial purposes—herein is to be
traced the conjectural opinion of the Convention in the matter
of Territories, and the sources of their formation—no settled
purpose or view, but merely anticipatory—North Carolina,
however, in 1789, in compliance with the suggestion made in
the Constitution, and in imitation of Virginia, from whom that
suggestion was taken, and who under the advice of the prophetic
Jefferson, ceded before the adoption of the Constitution,

it is not more properly advisory, than what is to be found in the 2d clause of the 3rd section, conferring upon Congress the power, in the exercise of the National Sovereignty over the Territories. "to dispose of and make all needful rules and regulations respecting them or other property belonging to the United States"—not defining what the rules and regulations were to be, with the same jealous care that, in the case of Federal and State Sovereignties, is observable, but requiring merely the agency of Congress in peculiarly adequate terms, and in true conformity to the different stage of political existence, to transact thus far the temporary and transient duties of the General Sovereignty in the Territories—the terms used, also, are of the most arbitrary import, as before observed, and plainly declare the different grade of political importance, in which the framers of the Constitution held the full grown rights of the Federal and State Sovereignties, and the infant tutelage of a Territory—there is nothing to be discovered in any degree of great importance being attached to these waste lands by the Nation in 1787, or in the fact that their political existence as Territories, if political existence it was to be, a matter then more of distant expectancy and hope, than of speedy or even approximate result, would be aught else than an organization non-essential and brief, to justify the Convention to make any reservations discriminating in favor of the Territories and against the unqualified Sovereignty of the Federal Government, on any subject of legislation either local or general—there is no special authority conferred upon the Federal Government by the agency of Congress to lay and collect taxes, duties, imposts and excises, to provide for organizing, arming and disciplining a militia, or other exalted Governmental Powers, and yet who will assert, that Congress the agent of the General Government, cannot exercise these powers in a Territory under the General Law—nor is there any special power granted to create a corporation or establish a ferry therein, and yet who denies the right of the agent Congress, or its sub-agent the Territorial Legislature, to pass such laws. There is nothing special legislatively given, and nothing special legislatively reserved in the Constitution in regard to the Territories, being the very reverse of the position of the Federal and State Governments, a proof irresistible that the legislative power of Congress over every subject matter of legislation, general or local, slavery inclusive, in the Territories, is the indisputable law of the Sovereignty.

Supposing that the term "State" was indiscriminately used, and that it occasionlly meant Territory as applied to Territory subsequently acquired, and not ceded by any of the original thirteen States, a very violent supposition, as put by Mr. Douglas, what was there in the condition of the existence of slavery in the Country in 1787, that would call for a special Constitutional reservation in its favor in the Territories, where it did not exist, when the institution, as it is now respectably called, was on the wane in the States where it did exist, and the limit of the importation of slaves, the source from which slavery was supplied, was even fixed in an Article signed in 1774, by the Delegates from all the Colonies, thus early taking the first determined step towards its final dissolution—for the flag of slavery has varied its elevation considerably, both in Colonial and Independent America, sometimes raised highly, especialy in the Colonies, when even Virginia denounced it, and again in 1787, after the Independence of the Country, aye the Country itself was conquered from England, trailing in the dust, the patriots and pure men of the land with General Washington at the head, as at the head of every other National Good, taking prudent measures for freeing the people from this last cruel vestige of British avarice and power—is it compatible, that reservations were entertained and duly weighed in the minds of the Convention, in favor of a vicious and unpopular system, and its special protection in wide spread wastes, where no slave to serve nor master to claim service from him dwelt, at a time when every prospect of its speedy dissolution was clear, when very many of the States were on the eve of taking decisive action on it, when the intent of individual manumission was openly expressed, as a public example and a private duty, by those eminent men in numbers, whose word was a fiat, is it reasonable to push conjecture to such verges, that construction can discover in the Constitution, framed by these men, protection and exemption in the Territories, for this nearly obsolete system of social debasement, when the language of the great instrument itself is strictly silent thereon; was a transient form of government ordained to possess permanent features, only in behalf of a dying system of social life, that was spurned by the Nation, not in the locality where it yet lingered, but where it was never yet introduced, and had very little prospect ever of a home ; was the Sovereignty of the Federal Government to be shorn of all its attributes in the Territories on the subject matter of slavery alone, when it exercised imperial sway without any Constitutional limit on every other subject matter of Legislation, local or national—the conclusion which every dispassionate man will arrive at is, that the framers of the Constitution taking no thought of slavery in the Territories, as they employed no language direct, granting to it freedom and reservation from Congressional action thereon, so did they not wrap up such intent in the plain and intelligible terms of the 1st and 2d clauses of the 3rd Section of the 4th Article of the Constitution—and that the inherent right of Sovereignty in the Federal Government over the Territories, and of legislation by Congress on all matters therein, slavery included, is not impinged by these or any other clauses of the instrument.

If Congress, Constitutionally, has the power of unlimited legislation in the Territories, the 3rd clause of the 2d Section of the 4th Article, respecting a fugitive from labor, is a very subordinate provision, out of which the ability or ingenuity of a Statesman or of any man, can evolve nothing of material import; it is a provision of detail, in terms the most discreet, and simply guards, that if a person owes labor, he shall not successfully avoid the payment of the debt, by fleeing from the State where the debt is due, or by being discharged from its payment by force of the law of the State to which he escapes, but shall be delivered up—this is its extent and no more, the sanction by the Constitutional Law of an act of comity between sister States, wherein the debt of a citizen of one of them is involved, and which, from its rare and extraordinary nature, being not money nor chattles of any kind, but the involuntary service of a human being, a laborer, to whom, however worthy, his hire is not paid, contrary to the doctrine of honesty, is capable of exit and escape, impelled by every instinct that drives us, and aided by the resources, how-ever limited, of the divine mind—it is an anomaly in the nature of claim, and so regarded by the Constitution in the terms that it employs, giving no precedence to that of the master in favor of slavery, over that of the slave in favor of freedom, for, among other things, the labor debt is to be first ascertained, and is a condition precedent to the delivery ; the interpretation that makes color presumptive evidence of slavery, and puts it to the proof of freedom or non-indebtedness of labor, is not patronized by the Constitution, but is one of these wolfish dogmas of the petty law, that its professors have in all time been prolific of inventing, with a few, very few honorable exceptions, who have sided with liberty ; the great majority, especially those eminent in rank, whether on or off the bench, being instinctively prone to aid and abet tyranny, and the ranker it is, the more ingenious and plausible the defences these men ever invent and surround it with. In the 3rd clause of the 2d Section, being the service or labor clause, no

encouragement or patronage is given in behalf of the expansion
of slavery in the States even, and very scanty is the countenance
it there receives to retain what it claimed—were it favored,
instead of being shunned, were it treated as a just right, instead
of a compulsory wrong, how differently would the Constitutional language declare itself—and least of all, can the faintest
reference to slavery in the Territories or the application of the
fugitive clause therein be traced—the provision, such as it is,
made in the Constitution restricting and directing States, over
which without this authority Congress could not afterwards
act, was deemed needful, whereas in the Territories, that the
Federal Government supremely ruled in virtue of its unrestricted sovereignty, Congress could at any time enact provision
on the subject of fugitive labor and its delivery."
    Reasoning similar hereto, but more comprehensive and
elaborate, always standing within the circle of the Constitution,
could be advanced by an intelligent and disinterested citizen,
as to the true import of these clauses—but such is the power
of passionate clamor, raised and kept up by the seductive
influence of the relation of master and slave, a love the more
bewitching the more it is illegitimate and unholy, that the
strained uses to which the plain language and import of the
Constitution have been put of late, are regarded by certain
men as no longer unnatural or dangerous—they are taken up
and coolly converted in the study of the Statesman, and the
chambers of the Judiciary—precedent has no force, and the
uniform course of legislation prepared and presided over by
Mr. Jefferson and Mr. Madison is slighted or belied by
metaphysical and legal subtlety, or bullied with the raw
dexterity of a western stump speech. How precipitately has
Mr. Douglas not fallen from the sublime, when, in one of his
vagaries in aid of this doctrine of Popular Sovereignty, he
invented in its support the other new doctrine of Sovereignty
in abeyance and in trust, a grand discovery, which places the
gentleman, as a jurist, at the head of this or any other age,
and which rebukes the wisdom of the Codes of all time—
would it not be well, that he be permitted to take unto himself
leisure and retirement, in order to perfect his treatise on the
unknown doctrine of Sovereignty in Abeyance, and bequeath
it to his country, a rarer inheritance than even any that may
unfortunately befal her from his Chief Executive occupations.
    Mr. Douglas has announced his Doctrine of Popular
Sovereignty in the Territories, as an invention of which he is
the first discoverer, and for which he claims a patent from the
people—he instinctively apprehended the plausibility of the

.